Shipping Container Homes

The best guide to building a shipping container home, including plans, FAQs, and much more!

Table of Contents

Introduction

Thank you for taking the time to pick up this book about Shipping Container Homes!

This book aims to educate you on shipping container homes, and how to begin designing and building your own! In the following chapters you will learn about the different types of containers, how to source them, what the building process entails, and much more.

At the completion of this book you will have a good understanding of container homes and have an idea as to whether this type of home is feasible for you. As you will soon discover, a range of permits and approvals may be required for you to build a container home in your area. Despite these potential challenges, shipping container homes provide many benefits in terms of cost, design, and sustainability!

Once again, thanks for choosing this book, I hope you find it to be helpful, and enjoy learning more about this fantastic type of housing!

Chapter 1: What Are Container Homes

With housing markets currently in a volatile state, people who are interested in home ownership rather than renting are becoming more innovative in their choice of shelter.

One mode of housing that is increasingly becoming popular makes use of shipping containers for its base structure. Indeed, shipping container homes have grown to become a more affordable, cost-effective, sustainable, and unique form of housing.

Shipping containers are commonly used to transport cargo across continents. These containers are built from reinforced steel, allowing them to function despite exposure to harsh weather conditions and heavy loads; not to mention rough handling across ports. And these features actually make them an excellent building material for houses.

Thousands, if not millions, of these containers are regularly manufactured every year to cater to a growing demand. Homeowners interested in having a shipping container home of their own can buy them new or second hand.

Regardless of being new or second hand, a wide variety of containers are always available to those who need them, and the price tag is relatively cheap compared to conventional building materials.

Not only is the cost rather enticing, but using these containers make for a greener approach to homebuilding as well. When old units are bought for the purpose of building a house, the steel is recycled without having to exert additional effort or burn through resources to melt it down. It significantly reduces one's carbon footprint, adding to its appeal for new age homeowners.

Although the space a shipping container provides can be quite limited, it has the feature of being open to modifications. A comfortable house can easily be made by combining several of these containers vertically or horizontally.

But different elements go into the construction process. Various costs come with this type of project. Throughout this book, you will find out more about these container units, how they function, and how they can readily be used to create a one-of-a-kind home.

Chapter 2: Permits, Laws, And Licenses

You need to prepare the materials that you will be using for the build, and this starts with checking building regulations in your area, securing the necessary permits, and hiring the necessary professionals to help you out.

Building a house from shipping containers does not make it less of a structure, and this is why permits and licenses are still necessary. You might encounter contractors or building agents that will suggest forgoing permits to cut costs. Although offers like these are somewhat attractive, it is a trap that you should not fall for.

The process of securing permits together with local building code compliance are two of the most challenging hurdles that come with building shipping container houses. Because of its relatively new concept, and also due to the highly specialized niche market, there is currently no clear-cut system in place in most areas.

Standard building practices are applied when this type of infrastructure is constructed. Before an occupancy permit is granted by local housing agency officials, the homeowner must meet basic health and safety standards for the project. Building plans should be presented for approval, and a final inspection is to be conducted after the build is completed.

When it comes to the building plans, it is possible for homeowners to draft these themselves as long as they meet the requirements of the local housing agency. In some cases, the absence of an architect's stamp may fly, but only for the initial draft. All plans for final approval must have the support and final outlay of a licensed architect lest they be rejected.

The stamp ensures that a licensed professional has seen the plans and is taking responsibility for the integrity and design of the structure about to be built. If something were to happen, accidents for example, as a result of these plans, all liabilities will befall on the architect. Shipping containers used for storage purposes don't require this stamp, but those to be used as homes do.

The need for permits may also stem from area classification. In most cases, permits are no longer needed in areas belonging to farm, ranch, or agricultural zones. Zoning is a matter that you need to pay attention to.

Each zone has a distinct set of building and occupancy regulations that should be followed to a T. Making the mistake of missing out on satisfying even a single rule can lead to the building being deemed unfit for use. Aside from hefty fines and penalties, the structure could be torn down.

A good thing about zones is that they are pretty easy to check. Simply pay the local building department a visit and have your zone verified right then and there. Aside from checking zones and the regulations that they come with, you can also ask the same agency whether or not shipping container homes can be used for building in the area.

They can also provide information on the specific permits needed for the construction if the zone allows for such infrastructures to stand. Be sure to note down who provided the information so that you have a name to mention should there be problems with regulations later on.

If you will be obtaining the services of a general contractor, he or she can process all permits and licenses on your behalf. You do have the option of obtaining your own building permits as well, but this will take time.

You can even choose to build the structure yourself but only do so if you possess the same level of skills as the local contractors, builders, draftsmen, and architects in your area. If not, it would be logical not to mention cost-effective to let the professionals handle this task.

With shipping containers, the ones used to make homes are usually pre-owned. Unless they are sourced brand new, the homeowner must also obtain the necessary clearance from the health department deeming the container clean and safe enough to be converted into a residential space.

Chapter 3: Sourcing Containers

Intermodal shipping containers are some of the most widely used cargo units around the world. These are made out of steel composite and come in various types, as well as sizes.

A huge chunk of the total number of available shipping containers around the globe are referred to as dry freight, which basically means that they are general purpose containers used to transport different dry materials or products across continents.

These durable steel boxes come with double ended doors which can be closed and sealed with ease. The standard lengths are either twenty or forty feet, with a height ranging from eight and a half to nine and a half feet. If necessary, an extender can be added to the top wall offering an additional foot of height per container.

An intermodal shipping container is one of the larger shipping boxes readily available today and is designed to cater to intermodal transport. It means that these boxes can be shipped via different modes of transportation including land, air, and sea.

Aside from this, the containers can be shipped without having to unload or reload cargo until they reach their final destination. Securing the boxes is easy as there are multiple locking systems in each one, with the final keys only available to the shipper or receiver.

Millions of these intermodal cargo units can be found around the world actively being used in the constant importation and exportation of goods and materials. Years after their inception, they have become the primary choice for carrying cargo as they allow for more effective and efficient transport.

You can get them from manufacturers if you're interested in brand-new containers. If your budget only allows for the clean, used variety, you can also get these from manufacturers, cargo lots, and even the companies that no longer have use for their inventory.

Without additional support pillars, standard containers that are the same size can be stacked one on top of the other. However, if they are different sizes, without modifications it is not safe to stack containers on top of one another.

It is always best to consult a structural engineer when it comes to something like this to ensure that the structure is balanced and safe for whatever purpose it intends to serve.

Chapter 4: Preparations To Make

Apart from acquiring the permits or licenses, you also have to source the shipping containers for your home. Other things that you have to concern yourself with include determining a working budget and deciding whether or not professionals should be consulted for the project. When it comes to the latter, they can help you with the different stages of the project from the design component to the build itself.

Depending on your skill level and knowledge when it comes to construction, apart from regular builders, you might also want to get the help of a licensed contractor. It is always a wise decision to consult a reliable home contractor when it comes to a build like this.

Choosing a quality professional can make a huge difference when it comes to a job done properly or an utter nightmare.

Sourcing through referrals is the best option here as people have had a first-hand experience as to the kind of work a contractor can provide. They have seen him at work and can provide a certain level of expectation. Start by consulting family, friends, and neighbors that have had construction work done recently.

Keep in mind that even if a contractor was referred to you, it is still necessary for you to run a complete background check and interview. It is a good idea to consider three to five potential applicants for your construction needs.

Doing so provides you with options especially since these professionals may come to offer varying skills and services, as well as at varying prices. The most challenging aspect of any build, for a homeowner, is not the work itself but locating a competent contractor who can deliver quality output in a timely manner.

When conducting your background check, work with local agencies, preferably those handling consumer affairs, or a chapter of the Better Business Bureau operating in your area. Check for blacklists, complaint histories, and the like.

Aside from checking a contractor's work history, check for licensing records as well. A contractor must pass a standard competency examination to be issued a license. The absence of this legal document also signals a red flag.

Keep in mind though that possessing a license does not equate with excellent workmanship. This is still something left for the client to decide. A license simply offers the sense of professionalism and commitment to the job at hand.

Insurance is essential. A contractor should be insured, and the homeowner should have ample insurance coverage as well. Coverage for physical injuries on site, property damage, and natural disasters are necessary. See to it that a working comprehensive policy is in order before any of the work begins.

Oftentimes, a construction project requires several contractors --- a general contractor and subcontractors working under his or her command. The number of contractors needed for a build depends on the size of the project and the requirements imposed upon by the homeowner.

A general contractor works by organizing the work schedule, securing the necessary permits, and coordinating with material suppliers. The subcontractors serve to handle specific elements of the build. One may be hired to handle all of the electrical work and utilities while another may be in charge of built-in furnishings or external landscaping.

In some cases, general contractors have teams of subcontractors that they can refer. If this network is unavailable, it will be the homeowner's responsibility to find these specialists one by one.

Searching for contractors is only one part of the equation. What follows is getting a bid from each prospect being considered. A written bid is necessary as it can be transformed into a binding contract. With any type of construction project, every correspondence has to be on paper.

Be sure to get bids covering the same job tasks or output, manpower requirements, material sourcing, and the like. This will make it easier for you to choose the best contractor to hire.

Engaging in price negotiations during the bidding process is fine as long as all requests from both parties are reasonable. All bids and negotiations should be finalized before any contract is signed, as altering parts of it later on can lead to more expenses on your part.

Just like any other product or service in the market, being cheap does not make it the best considerable option. In this line of work, price usually dictates quality. A home is something that is meant to last for a long time so paying a bit more for better output is worth doing.

By paying more, a homeowner will not only be entitled to a better effort from the builders, but better materials as well. Even if the costs are higher in the short run, the generated savings in the long run will usually be greater.

In negotiating a fair contract, make sure that the document spells out all the terms of the work involved as this will help both parties reduce or eliminate the occurrence of time-consuming and costly misunderstandings during the build. Here are the initial pieces of information that the contract should carry.

- Contractor's Professional Contact and Work Details

- Subcontractors' Professional Contact and Work Details

- Homeowners' Personal Details

- Project Timetable

- Payment Method and Schedule

- Scope of Work

- List of Specific Materials Needed

- List of Machinery and Equipment Needed

- Demolition and Clean-Up Details

- Terms of the Agreement

- Arbitration Provisions or Dispute Clauses

- Limitations of Liability for the Homeowner

- Insurance Details

- Date of Signing

- Signatures of All Parties Involved

- Addendum for Non-Inclusions to the Contract

Construction projects are normally done in phases, and payments follow suit as they are settled in stages over the course of the build. This includes the delivery of key supplies and materials. A contractor will usually require a down payment of about ten percent or so.

Protect yourself by not paying more than what is necessary during this stage. In most cases, even with initially trustworthy contractors, they have the tendency of using excess payments to finance projects of other clients oftentimes leaving the financier, you, high and dry as time passes.

Always be in communication with the contractors. Aside from receiving frequent project updates, this enables all parties to resolve problems as early as possible. Resolving issues during the course of the build is better than having to attend to them after the turnover.

Contractors, during the build, are keener on fixing problems like leaking roofs or faulty wiring and the like. Getting them to attend to these issues later on will be quite the challenge as they have already received payment for the initial service and won't be at a loss for the sloppy output.

A good security measure to ensure that you are extended reasonable aftercare services is to include a clause in the contract allowing you to hold the final payment installment for a month after the turnover.

Aside from ensuring that all construction as per your specifications is met a hundred percent, the full payment to the main contractor should only be given after you have obtained signed documents covering payments to subcontractors, suppliers, and other expenses for the build.

These official release papers are called mechanic's-lien waivers. They stand as receipts for services and products received. Without the formal release from obligation, these agencies can have a mechanic's lien placed against your house until all payables have been settled. Demand these waivers together with official receipts for all purchases and expenses from the general contractor.

Chapter 5: The Design Process

The Internet is an excellent place to start looking for ideas prior to the build. There are tons of free resources that can be accessed with the click of a button. Some, more professional, layouts may be obtained for a minimal fee.

Depending on the available square footage, homeowners can also focus their attention on developing a variety of living areas. These are the bedroom, bathroom, kitchen, and living room.

The amount of livable space may be quite limited depending on the type of container that's been chosen, how many containers there will be, and the dimensions of each one.

Because shipping container homes are unlike traditional houses in many ways, it is important for potential homeowners to be fully aware of the restrictions that may come with this choice of residence. Not only will there be a more limited amount of space to work with, but when container units are stacked, there is also a weight limit for the upper tiers.

When planning a shipping container home, everything should be decided according to the specific needs of the homeowner. A good move would be to work closely with an architect and interior designer who can provide the best insight as to how a space can be arranged to deliver an outcome that will be up to par.

When it comes to floor plans and design blueprints, homeowners will require the assistance of competent professionals. An architect, a structural engineer, and an interior designer can help determine the best placements for furnishings and divisions for rooms, not to mention identify where extra supports may be necessary. Landscapers can assist on the outside part of the home.

Generally, the living area should have the largest space allotment out of the four as it will be the place where the greatest amount of time will be spent. It could be best to combine the kitchen and living area into a free-flowing space which will also serve the purpose of acting as a convertible dining area.

The bedroom can also exist without a separate wall or door. In this case, it is a great idea to use simple wall dividers that can provide the necessary privacy, without taking up too much room in the modular unit.

Wall dividers can easily be positioned to increase or decrease the amount of available space in each area. If there is a room that needs the utmost privacy, it will be the bathroom. It would be best to secure this room with a lockable door, but to save space you could opt for sliding ones instead of traditional swivels.

To live comfortably despite a potentially smaller fixed space allotment, homeowners should be mindful not only of their choice of furniture but everything that they bring into the home.

If multiple shipping container units will be stacked atop one another, the assistance of a structural engineer should be attained. The structural engineer will be the one to assess the allowable weight limit for the tiers. In some cases, additional support beams or posts may be installed at the bottom tier to make the upper units as functional and safe as possible.

Chapter 6: The Building Process

It is important that any dirt, dust, or debris is removed from the container. Abrasive materials, bristled brooms, and the like may be used for this process. If a pressure washer is available, then use it to greatly expedite the cleaning process. It would be best to get the help of a professional when it comes to any pressure washing as the process can overwhelm a non-expert.

Start at the end of the container moving your way towards the main doors. Pay a lot of attention to the seams, the nooks, and all the crannies you see. Check the floors for wear and tear as well. Excessive damage should raise a red flag.

Start cleaning the inside, then move your way out of the container. If a pressure washer is used, it may be powerful enough to strip off any old paint not to mention rust that has formed on the steel. Any excess corrosion that cannot be initially removed can be treated with acidic compounds like vinegar.

To hasten the process, rub the vinegar in using pieces of aluminum foil. Depending on the gravity of the rust situation, industrial cleaners may also be used. If the corrosion is excessive and has caused other, more serious, damage to the unit, it may be best to simply forego the particular container.

After it dries, do a secondary cleaning run by going over the container with some medium grit sandpaper on a belt or orbital sander. This serves the purpose of removing any remaining paint flakes. You do not have to strip off all of the old paint, just the areas which show signs of wear because if you don't, the new paint that you apply will peel off in no time.

Prime the container to seal it against corrosion and any moisture. You can then apply any paint color of your choosing to the interior and exterior walls of the shipping container.

If the builder needs to cut portions out of any side walls, the cutting and sanding should be done prior to the priming and painting. This will save the builder a lot of time and money. When choosing paints, thicker solutions work best for steel shipping containers. Not only do they offer stronger and longer-lasting external seals, but thick paints also stick better to the metal structures.

Before general construction begins, obtain all necessary permits and source materials from reliable suppliers. Also form a team of laborers depending on the magnitude of the task at hand. If a contractor is hired, he or she will be the one to handle these.

General construction begins with site work. This involves finding a designated location for the shipping container home. This is the time for groundwork. It may necessitate some excavation to lay the foundation in. At this time, plans for utilities, water management, and septic systems must also be laid out.

The size of the main ground foundation depends on how many containers are included in the design plans and how much weight is expected to be held after construction is completed. The foundation should be strong enough to keep everything in place even when disasters like typhoons or earthquakes hit.

The foundation can be built using precast concrete panels to make things easier for the builder. If a homeowner can afford the time, a stronger foundation can be created using hollow cement blocks and poured concrete.

This goes atop an excavated area that can be filled with gravel to assist with drainage. As the foundation is laid out, builders can add insulating elements and water proofing components for a better final structure.

The process of setting the building's foundation is the trickiest step in the project because it must also address gas supply lines, utilities, and electrical wiring components. These are run from the base of the foundation to their respective positions in the home's floor plan.

After all of these are taken care of, there is the matter of sealing the main foundation. Traditional methods make use of compacted soil, gravel, laid-out rebar, and more concrete on-pour.

Shipping containers have been designed to carry a modular outlay, but these bodies can be modified to fit the needs of the homeowner. Although the corrugated steel walls have been fabricated to support heavy loads, not to mention constant exposure to the elements, these can be cut to specifications with the proper equipment.

In cases where modular units are placed side by side, not simply stacked atop one another, openings for internal entryways and windows can be cut into the units.

When it comes to these types of modifications, simple as they may seem, it would be best for professionals to be called in for assistance. Aside from an expert builder, a structural engineer, and an architect should also be contacted.

This is because removing a portion of any wall or corner can significantly weaken the structure, reducing the weight that its roof can support. Aside from steel-cutting, welding and framing are other elements involved in the general construction of shipping container homes.

Although these are important parts of the project, they can come at an expense and this is why modifications should only be done when extremely necessary.

After the foundation sets and the container units are prepared for final assembly, it is time to secure them to the foundation and each other. Each base unit is to be crane-lifted onto the foundation, hooked, and welded down. Because of the weight of these container units, it does not take much to secure them into place.

Corner fasteners are all that is necessary to hold them onto the foundation. Additional support can be installed through the use of corner concrete blocks. Containers can then be secured to one another, vertically or horizontally, by making welds. If several units are to be stacked atop one another, additional support beams as dictated by the structural engineer should be utilized.

Internal and external entryways, windows, and other openings should then be framed. The most common method used by builders for shipping container homes begins with steel frames which are then reinforced by wooden ones.

Because of the limited amount of living space provided by cargo units, sliding doors and windows are commonly used. In this case, the steel and wood double frames can be made to run on wheels through L-section panels.

The house is now ready for insulation to be installed. Utility systems and electrical wiring are also run through the home at this point. When the walls have been sealed and all finishes completed, interior plans from painting, to furniture arrangements, to the installation of fixtures can then be satisfied.

Depending on the location, external landscaping may be necessary to add to the home's aesthetic value. Everything then need to go under inspection before a certificate of occupancy can be attained. Homeowners that have adequate skills in building can tackle a project like these themselves but for most, the best route is to go with professional laborers.

Chapter 7: Foundation Types

One of the most important things that you have to consider when building a shipping container home is choosing the correct foundation. This will ensure that your home will last and be safe to live in for years to come.

For those who are new to this type of home concept, yes, it requires a stable foundation as it still needs to literally be housed down. Even if you don't notice it, the ground moves. Without the right foundation, your home can sink or slide. Even the slightest of movements can affect your home's levelling.

A foundation serves to provide a stable anchor; a platform if you will. Apart from ensuring that your home stays in place, it reduces the potential onset of the containers separating; or worse, splitting.

Now there are different types of foundations that you can choose from. The best option will depend on your type of shipping container home, and the ground you want to build it on.

Usually, you'll be dealing with combinations of various materials, like rock and clay for example. The differences in texture and strength will affect the evenness of your home. An uneven home can pose problems like doors that won't open properly.

When you build a shipping container home on a foundation, you can ensure that the home is stable and the weight inside is distributed evenly. Apart from these factors, having a solid foundation also reduces the onset of corrosion as moisture is more properly controlled.

The thing about foundations Fons though is that they're ideal for homes that you're planning on installing permanently in a specific location. If you're planning on moving after several months or after a couple of years, it'd be better if you just use railroad ties.

What Types of Foundations are Available?

For shipping container homes, there are typically three main types of foundations that people choose from:

- **Pier Foundation**

What you have here are the most commonly chosen foundations for shipping container homes. For one, they are extremely affordable. Even non-professionals can install them. And they are quite easy to construct.

With a pier foundation, your solid base will be a series of concrete blocks. These blocks are referred to as the piers. On average, every block will measure in at 50 cubic centimeters. Several of these blocks are laid side by side on each corner of a shipping container home.

Depending on how large the container is, it's possible for the contractor to use two or three levels of bricks to allow for an even sturdier foundation. When it comes to these bricks, you don't really need to use any special equipment during the build. You don't even have to do any excavation work.

- **Slab Foundation**

There are times when the ground is made out of softer materials. In this case, you need the kind of foundation that will allow for a better and more equal distribution of weight. This is where the slab foundation enters the scene.

Unlike a pier foundation, you need to excavate the ground to install a slab foundation. You need to excavate at least 18 square feet of land area. Concrete will then be poured into this hole, then after it dries, you can then put the shipping container home on top; securing it in place with heavy-duty metal bearings.

The size of the slab needs to be larger than the home. Usually, contractors extend the foundation at least 2 feet longer than the container. But this also means that the homeowner will end up spending more money on it compared to pier foundations.

Slab foundations are beneficial because they provide a sturdy and solid base without any hollow spaces in-between. This helps reduce the onset of termite infestations. But you have to fix any underground utility lines prior to the concrete drying.

You should see to it that these are made accessible before the foundation sets or else you've lost access for good.

- **Strip Foundation**

The strip foundation combines both the pier and slab foundations. It also goes by another name – the trench foundation. It's not a full slab of concrete, but is also not just made out of corner ballasts.

It's a concrete strip that measures around 2 by 4 feet that can go around the perimeter of shipping container homes.

It's a less expensive option compared to the slab foundation, but requires a harder base surface. It's best used on areas that are hit by significant rainfall. This is because there'll be enough space for the water to run through and be drained away.

If there's a downside to this type of foundation, it's that it can be rather weak in the face of heavy winds and earthquakes. This is because of their shallow form. Also, this type of foundation is ideal for smaller-scale shipping container homes.

Attaching Shipping Containers to the Foundation

Regardless of the type of foundation that you choose, attaching the container itself involves a relatively similar process across the board. Usually, the best connector to use is a steel plate. Especially when you're working with concrete, you can set these plates before anything dries. Install them with the help of some vertical bars for added support.

Once the concrete dries and cures, you can then place the containers atop, and weld on additional supports to the steel plate. But do know that this isn't the only option that you have. You can choose not to use steel plates and instead bolt the containers down into place with the help of some concrete anchors. This is simpler, but the first option provides a much more durable foundation.

Chapter 8: Insulation Types

There are different types of insulation that homeowners can consider. The final choice will depend on the area they chose to live in, how cold the temperature can get, and of course, the overall project budget.

Environmentally friendly alternatives to traditionally manufactured insulation products are readily available these days and offer the same benefits without leaving a massive carbon footprint. This chapter will discuss some examples of commonly used insulation materials and methods that are greener in nature.

A living roof is not exactly a roof that is alive. It is not a direct form of insulation as well. What it is, is a design element that helps the homeowner control temperatures within the home. It is a moving, convertible roof that can be repositioned during the summer months and reverted back when the rainy season kicks in. It is best described as a sloped roof.

During the summer months, the hot air that builds up in the home is allowed to escape. Any cool air is then allowed into the container as it gets pushed in through the roof. It follows the concept of hot air rising and cold air sinking. This can be used together with basic home insulation to give the homeowner better control over temperatures in a shipping container abode.

Cotton insulation is another spin-off of the blanket type insulation product. In this case, what replaces the fiberglass or rock wool is a bunch of recycled clothing. Just like sheep's wool, cotton is a naturally-occurring product.

It is a renewable resource that can be grown in a short span of time, making it an ideal component for such an in-demand product. Unlike sheep's wool though, cotton is fairly expensive so unless a builder plans on using old clothes in the process, the synthetic option may be better.

The past years have seen the rise of mud as an excellent material that can be used to build homes on its own. For those who do not plan on living in a mud-brick house, the same material can be used for insulation instead.

It is best applied to shipping container homes that will be positioned in locations where the climate is not only hot, but dry as well. It has the capacity to keep heat out and retain a cool internal temperature.

For typical homes, the mud is simply padded onto the walls and allowed to dry and set. In the case of shipping container homes, the mud can be cladded onto the external walls and roofing.

Since the container is made out of steel, the builder will have to use battens as these will keep the mud in place. Battens refer to a solid strip of material usually fabricated from plastic, metal, or fiberglass. Mud insulation is not ideal for areas where there is frequent rainfall, as excess moisture is its weakness.

Most comparable to blanket insulation is the eco-friendly wool variety. It follows a relatively similar concept. The only difference is that instead of fiberglass or rock wool, sheep's wool is used to create the blanket.

It reduces one's carbon footprint because it reduces the need to manufacture the synthetic materials. It utilizes natural sheep's wool, making it a sustainable and naturally-occurring product.

One of the best but most costly types of insulation is that of the spray foam variety. It is expensive because it is extremely simple to apply. You just spray it to the desired spot from a can and you are good to go.

As it leaves the vacuum of the spray can, the closed-cell polyurethane foam expands and hardens taking the shape of wherever it was sprayed on. This means that it can get into the tightest nooks and crannies of a structure, creating a seamless barrier as it hardens into place.

As no space is left uncovered, no air pockets or gaps are left. Air pockets are the primary origin of corrosion and mold-causing moisture and bacteria. Aside from being the easiest to use, it is readily available and provides the highest rating based on industry standards. The rating quality given to insulating materials are based on qualities including their ability to resist heat flow.

Roll, also referred to as blanket insulation, is commonplace in the construction industry. It is the cheapest of all available insulation materials on the market. Just like panel insulation, it calls for stud walls and can only be placed within these confines. These normally come fabricated from rock wool which is a mineral compound, or fiberglass.

Common and extremely user-friendly for DIY-ers is the panel insulation variety. Panels can be bought at hardware and construction depots and can be bought in various sizes or dimensions. There are predefined sizes available for sale, or builders can have these specially cut to size to suit their design plans.

Chapter 9: Roof Types

You've probably seen shipping container homes made completely out of containers. And then there are those that are equipped with roofing much like your typical house. In this case, the option to add a roof depends entirely on your preference and budget.

You don't need to add a roof to your home. This will save you from construction costs. But over time, you might require additional insulation as a result; and this will cost money. Depending on where you're residing, not having a roof may also result in higher energy bills.

This is why you have to weigh the pros and cons of installing a roof. Keep in mind that containers are made out of metal that conducts heat. Hot air rises. Without a roof, this air can easily escape. If you live in a cooler area, you might need help with keeping the heat in; and vice versa.

As you make a decision on whether or not to add a roof to your shipping container home, remember that a roof stands as additional insulation. It won't just keep the heat in, but it will also help keep the internal temperature consistent. Apart from this, it also helps manage rainfall, reducing potential costs when it comes to installing drip bars around the home's perimeter.

What Types of Roofing are Available?

There are three main types of roofing that you can choose from. Again, your choice will depend on your preference and budget.

- **Shed Roofing**

A shed roof is a common option for shipping container homes as it makes it appear as close to a traditional home as possible.

This is a sloped roof that's quite affordable to install. It's also quite easy to build. All it takes is a couple of days for everything to be set up. If the homeowners decide to install solar panels, this roofing option is the best choice as it provides the right angle for the panels to absorb maximum sunlight.

The installation process for this type of roof is quite simple. All you have to do is weld several right-angled steel plates across the length of the container on both sides. To add support, install a wooden beam underneath the overlapped plates and screw the trusses into it. You can add even more support with the help of some purlins or steel bars attached across the trusses.

If you can, work with a structural engineer for this project. This professional will help guide you when it comes to the load capacities of your shipping container home. As a result, you can rest assured that your roof won't damage the structure of the shipping container by being too heavy. This considers additional weight from rain, snow, or any other potential debris.

You can use galvanized metal sheets or traditional shingles aside from steel plates if you wish. Again, it all boils down to your preference and budget.

- **Gable Roofing**

Another type of roof that you can install is the gable. The steps are pretty similar to what has already been described with the shed roof, but this option focuses more on achieving a heightened degree of ventilation.

With the gable roof, slots are normally cut out of the steel plates or shingles. A disc cutter can be used for this task. In doing so, you're allowing the right amount of air to pass through the material. As a result, you reduce the onset of heat traps as well as condensation. Aside from having better control over the internal temperature, you're also reducing rust (due to condensation) from forming.

With this kind of roofing, you can improve the functionality and strength of the trusses by attaching a soffit board or fascia underneath them. But make sure there's an air gap measuring at least an inch wide in the middle. Cover this gap with some wire mesh and you'll be good to go. Air will flow through, but debris will be filtered out.

- **Flat Roofing**

When it comes to a flat roof, it's generally having a roof that's parallel to the topmost part of the shipping container. Think of it as a cover for a cooking pot. For some people, this type of roof may seem redundant, but in some cases, it simply offers added protection for the structure. It's the cheapest option available but is susceptible to having water pool on top of it.

The good thing about a flat roof is that it doesn't need to be made out of shingles, metal, or steel. Since it only acts as a safety barrier for the original roof of the container, all you really need is a literal cover. For most people, they use tarpaulin. Some weigh it down with asphalt. What this will do is protect the container's roof from being exposed to too much sunlight or rain; which can damage the metal material over time.

But you'll need the help of a structural engineer when it comes to roof installation. You could do the installation yourself, but you do need a professional who can help you assess the load that the container can carry on top.

The structural engineer will calculate how much material the roof of the container home can handle. He will also factor in the weight of those who'll construct the roof (as they need to, at some point, be on the roof themselves).

They will also take into consideration the elements (rain, wind, and snow) as well as the force of gravity to determine the container roof's load capacity. You need to make sure that the roof won't collapse during or after the installation.

Now, do understand that these calculations will vary from location to location. There are places that are prone to excessive rains, while others are susceptible to high winds. Given that there's no fixed standard on this sort of thing, you need to work with someone who's highly familiar with the local conditions to best identify the structural capacity.

So when you think about roofing, always identify what it is that you specifically need. Some homes require structural protection, while others need additional insulation. Work with a pro to help you figure out the other details of your build. Then choose the best type of roof that suits your individual needs and budget.

Chapter 10: How Much Will It Cost?

The cost of this kind of home depends primarily on what type of, and how many, shipping containers will be used during construction.

These can be bought new or used. New ones definitely cost more while used container units can be bought for three thousand dollars on average, typically. What homeowners get for this amount is a complete structure readily available for modification.

Made out of solid steel and welded together in the best possible way, these structures are extremely durable and offer an excellent yet cost-effective base or foundation for a house meant to be lived in for years.

An architect was able to construct a 2000 square foot home from six shipping containers. The total cost of the shipping container house from the cargo units to the modifications, insulation, finishes, furnishings, and other design elements only amounted to $120,000 which is pretty cheap compared to traditional houses on the market.

The only catch with shipping container homes is that more often than not it is the homeowner who must own the land that it resides on. Aside from purchasing the container units and spending on the land, homeowners must also shoulder various costs which include the securing of permits, electricity grid connections, and gas connections to name a few.

Depending on the homeowner, he or she can reduce the carbon footprint even more by installing solar panels on the home. A basic solar setup will cost about five thousand dollars depending on how green a homeowner wants to go.

There are people who live completely off the grid and have a complex solar panel setup in their shipping container home.

Although it may come at a large initial expense, it generates an excess of savings over time.

With this type of home, it can be built in a relatively short period of time. This means that labor expenses usually measure to about a third of what a traditional house may cost to build or renovate.

The thing about shipping container homes is that they can be built off-site and delivered to the final location ready to be lived in. If this is the option chosen by the homeowner, he or she should add the corresponding shipping costs to the total expense. Depending on how far the delivery point is, this can amount to several thousand dollars of additional expense.

Here are some of the common costs you should expect when it comes to this type of project:

- Steel Containers

- Foundation Prep

- Assembly and Modification of Units

- Installation Services

- Plumbing

- Electricity

- Roofing

- Flooring

- Furnishings

- Entryways

- Landscaping

- Finishing Work

Chapter 11: Cool Design Ideas

Here are some organizational and design hacks that will be well worth learning about. Not only will they allow for a cleaner looking space but over time, they will help homeowners focus more on what they need instead of what they simply want.

Bedroom

The bedroom is one of the most, if not the most, important part of any home as it offers a place for rest, relaxation, and refuge. This is why it should be kept organized at all times. Although clutter does foster creativity, it keeps the mind awake and alert.

At the time when a person only wants nothing but to rest, this is not the best thing in the world, for the brain to remain active when it should not be. Especially in a standard shipping container home where space allotment is typically quite limited, using the right furnishings and keeping personal belongings intact is highly necessary.

In the bedroom, the essential pieces of furniture include the bed, a closet, and a bedside table. These days, there are plenty of available sources for multi-functional furniture. This can mean having storage underneath the bedframe, a nightstand that can function as transformable seating, and a closet that can have a built-in dresser.

When it comes to the bedroom, it is important to keep things orderly. The minute a fresh batch of laundry comes in, immediately put the items in the closet. Do not leave the task for later. More often than not, you will tend to push it further into the future until your clothes are left in a corner.

Be mindful of floor space. Always keep in mind that if it can be stored, keep it out of sight, and if it can be hung, keep it off of the floors. A number of excellent lighting and ventilation fixtures can be screwed onto the walls giving a stylized effect while helping maintain the vision of a large floor area.

To further maximize the space and keep the bedroom serene, be selective when it comes to the choice of color. Go with light pastels or calming earth tones like tans and greys. Accent it with white or cream molding for an elegant overall look.

Keep the window treatments as simple as you can, but never ignore function. These should be thick enough to keep most of the light out, but not too thick that they make the space look smaller than it actually is.

Living Area

The living area will surely be the busiest part of the house. It will also be the primary area where homeowners will entertain visitors and guests over time.

This is the reason why, even with a limited amount of space, ample seating may be required. It is a good thing that there are plenty of furniture offerings these days that allow for multiple functionalities.

The living area is where the entertainment section should be. This may include a television set and its accompanying sound system, and video playback equipment. Depending on the homeowner type, video game consoles might also be a part of the equation.

Flat screen television sets are all the rage these days and in a shipping container home, these are ideal because they carry a sleek design and can easily be mounted to the wall.

Traditionally, sound system speakers, game, and video consoles are kept in an entertainment cabinet. If you can find one that does not occupy that much space, this is one of the easiest organizational options available today.

Having a lax budget means you can even have one built for your house suiting your specifications to a T. To make the process simpler, vie for hanging shelves instead. These are strong, durable, and can be hung in any way the homeowner pleases.

Again, by taking advantage of and maximizing the available vertical space, you can keep things off of the floors and maximize the visible horizontal area in your shipping container home. If the wall structure permits, all wiring can be drawn through the walls into a common exit point, lessening the look of clutter from multiple cords.

A comfortable sofa is important. Since the area will be the busiest one in the home, there should be no question when it comes to the need to invest in good furniture. If you are the type of homeowner who frequently has guests stay over, it could be a good idea to purchase a convertible sofa bed.

It can work well as seating during the day but also allows you to provide a cozy bed for people staying overnight. The best part is that the bed can conveniently be tucked back into place after usage.

Additional seating and storage can be provided by box ottomans. These can also double as end tables for the living room. Simply position a piece of glass or wood atop it, and you have a makeshift coffee table centerpiece. When it comes to lighting fixtures, suspended varieties work best.

Kitchen

In a shipping container home, it is important for sufficient ventilation to be applied to the kitchen area, especially if homeowners are active cooks. With the help of a structural engineer, several windows can be cut from the steel cargo unit and replaced with efficient exhaust systems. This is a very important initial step that should never be ignored.

When the ventilation has been taken care of, homeowners should then address the function of the kitchen. Will it be used solely for cooking and food preparation or will it double as a breakfast nook, if not a dining area as well? If the space will only be used as a designated kitchen for cooking, then homeowners should invest in the appliances that they need.

Most home kitchens come equipped with a stove top, an oven, an overhead exhaust, a microwave, a toaster, and a coffee maker. It sounds like a lot, but these are the basic appliances that go into a typical kitchen. If the allotted space and budget allows for all of these to be purchased, then by all means purchase them.

If the homeowner wants to keep the space simple but still have that food prep function then the toaster, coffee maker, and microwave may be scraped off from the list. It is fairly easy to heat meals, boil water for coffee, and toast bread on the stove top.

The necessity of the stove top and oven is self-explanatory. As for the overhead exhaust, in addition to the kitchen windows and general exhaust system, it will easily help homeowners control food smells that can penetrate walls and furniture.

It also works tremendously well in controlling the excess heat that may circulate around the kitchen and the shipping container home. As it is positioned directly above the stove top, it can immediately absorb the emitted heat and food smells while the homeowner cooks.

If the kitchen will double as a dining area, sufficient dining and seating provisions should be considered. This means that homeowners should invest in a table, for starters. If there is a limited amount of space to work with, a kitchen island can work well as a preparation area and dining table in the kitchen.

A makeshift bar can also be considered in this case. It can easily double as a room partition and the homeowner can take advantage of its multi-functionality. The number of chairs depends on how many people live in the home.

Usually, four seats are the standard. If there is enough space to work with, this can be extended to eight, followed by a round table that can be used to entertain guests. If the available space is limited, two to four chairs will work just fine.

Provided that there are multi-function pieces of furniture in other areas of the house, like the living room perhaps, these could then be used for extra seating when needed.

Next are the pots and pans. A home cook will surely love to have an assortment of pots and pans in different sizes, but an excess of these items can lead to clutter, not to mention unnecessary spending.

Instead of purchasing a number of these, consider investing in three to five kinds, but those of excellent quality. Not only will they last longer but they will take up less space in the kitchen as well. Keep in mind that these will be used one to a couple at a time so there really is no need to have tons of them lying around the house.

The same goes for plates, glasses, mugs, utensils, and cutlery. Only purchase what is necessary. If there will be a party at the house, consider getting their disposable counterparts. Not only are these affordable, but cleanup will also be a breeze. Just chuck them in the trash after use and you are good to go.

Do not forget about the pantry. Every kitchen must have a pantry to store various ingredients and ready-to-eat food items in. The pantry environment should be dry and cool as to keep food fresher for a longer period of time.

In a shipping container home, a pantry can be built into the structure much like a bedroom closet. When homeowners go for built-in storage, they can easily maximize the vertical space allotment in their homes.

Further increase the amount of available storage by having retractable shelving installed in the main pantry cabinet. This will make for more storage that can be accessed with ease. Just a quick pull will give homeowners access to the ingredients that they need for the meal they are preparing.

Bathroom

The rule of thumb for bathrooms is that they should be kept as simple as possible, while still being able to satisfy all of the homeowners needs. There are only four components necessary to make a bathroom complete:

- Sink

- Toilet

- Shower Area

- Storage

For most people, the sink is the first thing they use when they enter the bathroom upon waking up. They wash their face, brush, and floss their teeth, and proceed with their daily regimen from there. There is really no need to spend a lot of money on a sink because it provides a fairly basic function.

The important component that homeowners should pay attention to is the faucet. This fixture is important as it controls the amount of water being pumped into the sink.

A long-headed, curved faucet works best by offering a substantial amount of space between the water source and the sink. This extra space makes it easier for homeowners to wash their face, collect water, and the like. It allows for less water wastage too. For the knobs, go with the traditional spin knobs instead of the variety that runs on sensors.

Unlike the sink, it will be a wise decision to spend a bit more on the toilet fixture. This need to be durable enough to handle the daily wear and tear, and should be large enough to offer a comfortable experience to those using it.

Aside from the size and quality of the toilet, homeowners should also invest money in the flushing system. These days, there are multiple mode systems that help conserve water.

These come with two to three buttons. Each button is designated to release a certain amount of water when pressed so homeowners do not have to resort to a full flush, one that empties the entire water reservoir, every single time.

There is a new product that aims to help homeowners save even more water in their bathrooms. It is a combined sink and toilet setup. The way it works is that the faucet is linked to the main water line ,while the sink is connected to the toilet water reservoir.

Homeowners get a gush of clean water from the faucet which they can use as they please. The used water then flows down the drain of the sink into a pipe that is connected to the toilet water reservoir filling it with used water. There is no need to waste clean water to flush the toilet. As the reservoir fills up, this used water can then be recycled as flushing water.

Homeowners that have ample space and a higher working budget can equip their shipping container home with a bathtub and shower setup. For those who only have the option of choosing one of these, normally they will go for the traditional shower.

This part of the bathroom is pretty simple to address. All that is needed is enough space for a person to move in. It would be best to apply tiles to the designated area from the floor to about a half of the wall. This allows for easy maintenance. The tile also protects the outer wall from excess water exposure.

To control water flow, have a half-foot barrier built on the floor separating the shower area from the rest of the bathroom. Use either a shower curtain or a glass partition to complete the look.

Finally, a complementary feature to any bathroom at home is the storage cabinet for towels and toiletries. A common practice is having a shelf or two installed underneath the sink, again utilizing the available vertical space to save on the horizontal area.

If there is ample ceiling space, homeowners can also choose to have a cabinet built from the ceiling down to about a third of the total wall. The cabinet is meant for towels, paper napkins, toiletries, and all other products needed for a bathroom.

Home Office

A home office has a specific function just like other areas of the house. There are homeowners who have this in their houses, while others simply add a working desk to their living area for such a purpose.

If a homeowner has the space and budget for a designated home office, it can be designed in such a way that all of the things necessary to have a functional office are made available, but arranged neatly allowing for a compact space.

A good working desk is important in any home office. This should be large enough to fit a laptop, pens, notepads, and the like. If possible, go for a desk that has drawers underneath. Not only will these allow for more storage, but they will also help keep items intact and organized.

For most people, a significant amount of time is spent in a home office. This is why a good and comfortable chair is also worth the investment. An ergonomic chair should be considered as it offers excellent support for the back.

Invest in a good computer as well. Desktop computers are still popular, but for a compact home office, portable gadgets work best. In this case, investing in a quality laptop computer is a better direction to take.

The great thing about a laptop computer, aside from being able to fit inside a desk drawer, is that it can be taken to and from the shipping container home without much of a hassle. It allows for remote work to be possible whenever necessary.

Often taken for granted, a dedicated desktop lamp is also essential when it comes to any home office setup. Even if the room already houses lighting fixtures, there are times when these are not enough to provide the necessary lighting for a desk. There are small table lamps that can readily be bought, and they are not that expensive making them an excellent addition to any home office.

Outside

For the outside part of the home, basic landscaping can do a lot of good. Removing weeds, trimming the hedges, and watering the external part of the home is typically all it takes to maintain it, keeping it as clean as possible and preventing pests and similar nuisances.

The external part of the shipping container home does not require as much maintenance as the inside, but it should not be taken for granted. It significantly improves the aesthetic quality of the home, and structurally, maintaining the outer walls prevents any unforeseen issues from happening like the development of rust or structural imbalance, foundational problems, and so on and so forth.

Maintaining the yard is quite simple. Maintaining the structure itself requires a bit more effort. To keep the outer walls of the shipping container clean, weekly hosing is all it takes. To prevent the onset of unwanted rust, make sure that it dries completely after washing.

If necessary, grab a cloth to dab out any excess moisture, especially from the nooks and crannies of the container unit. A semi-annual touch up of primer, paint, and sealant will help maintain the container's aesthetic value while protecting it from the wear and tear of the elements.

As for the foundation, have it inspected at least once a year. In some cases, it might require patching or reinforcing. A contractor can help homeowners sort things out. Especially in areas where there is excessive rainfall or extreme heat, the foundation should not go unaddressed.

It is always better to take care of issues while they are young and require minimal repair, than having to worry about them when they are already full-blown as this will incur more costs, not to mention more stress for the homeowner.

Chapter 12: Where To Get Building Plans

If you're interested in building a shipping container home for yourself, do know that there are plenty of accessible resources these days. You can start your search for building plans by going online. There are construction sites and professional web pages on the topic. Most of them also have layouts that you can download to help you get started.

There are also people with such homes of their own that share designs on art boards like Pinterest or social platforms like Instagram. You'll find a lot of building plans here including blueprints for external structures, and internal designs. And the great thing about these resources is that they're often free, they offer variety, and they can be accessed with a few clicks of a button.

If you're interested in a more traditional route then you can consult with professional engineers, contractors, or architects who can draft a design for you based specifically on your needs and preferences. These experts can even give you sound advice on the best type of containers to use and structure to consider.

Shipping container homes are becoming more popular these days and so the amount of information that you'll be able to find will be relatively endless.

Chapter 13: Pros & Cons Of Container Homes

Before understanding how a shipping container home can benefit you, it is important to be mindful of the disadvantages that often come with this type of home. This starts with challenging temperature and humidity control.

Shipping containers are made entirely out of steel, and metals are known to be excellent conductors of heat. If used in areas where daily temperatures reach high levels, the experience can truly be a discomfort. When used in areas where temperatures tend to fall quite fast, the container can become extremely cold in an instant.

Containers call for a little bit more than basic insulation to combat extreme weather conditions. In some cases, multiple layers of insulating materials including brick, wood, and padding may be required if the shipping containers will be utilized for residential purposes.

Because the steel absorbs heat and cold fairly easily, temperature changes can easily cause moisture to over-develop. Given the isolated space, water beads can make the environment clammy. If left unattended to, rust will start to form. The problem with rust is that the minute it starts developing, it will continue to do so, slowly inching its way across the steel frame of the cargo unit.

Design limitations are another con when it comes to these types of homes. Although one of the advantages of shipping containers is that they can be stacked together to allow for a larger living area, the problem with these cargo units is that although they can be stacked, builders are limited to containers of a default dimension. If these containers are to be opened at one side and connected horizontally, it will take an additional amount of time, effort, and expense.

Container homes can be constructed on or off site but there is a catch. Given the significant size of the units, they need to be transported using heavy machinery like forklifts and cranes. If the intended space where the home is to reside cannot accommodate the large equipment, there is no way for the container units to be transferred or delivered.

There are also certain building regulations that bind these structures. Building regulations depend on the area, zone, and purpose. There are certain rules which restrict the types of homes that can be built per location. Shipping container homes are not allowed in certain cities or neighborhoods, so this can be a problem for the homeowner.

Securing a permit for construction may be close to, if not, impossible. It would be best to consult with the local housing authorities on whether or not the idea is feasible for a particular area before beginning the design process. Aside from container units per se, some places do not allow steel buildings to be built, so this is another concern that has to be addressed.

Because of the nature of the material used in making shipping container homes, there are certain locational regulations that demand flooring to be treated with specialized insecticides prior to the installation of wooden flooring, tiles, or carpets.

For shipping containers, the floors should be treated with a copper, chromium, and arsenic solution to kill off and prevent bacterial growth over time. If the floor area is not made of steel, any layering should be removed completely and disposed of prior to human habitation.

And unless you are working with a brand-new shipping container, cargo spillage will always be an issue that you have to address early on during your build. Shipping containers are used to transfer various products across borders. In some cases, they carry non-perishable items but there are instances when they are used for perishable food products, not to mention cargo that may be of a radioactive or dangerous nature like chemicals for example.

Spillage cannot be prevented at all times, so contaminants, some of which are undetectable, may leak onto the container. If a homeowner does not ensure proper cleansing prior to the build, this can lead to extreme and costly repercussions later on. Significant expense is necessary to clean a shipping container as abrasive cleansing is needed, as well as sealant application.

Shipping containers are manufactured to cater to the purpose of storage or the transport of goods across countries. They are not designed to be lived in, so most manufacturers make use of standard materials and solvents in the fabrication process. There are solvents used in painting or sealing the steel that can be harmful to humans even after they dry up. Again, to make a cargo unit suitable for living in, the steel should be stripped raw using abrasive materials and toner sealants.

A used shipping container, before it is used to make a home, may also suffer from expected weathering and structural damage. Even the strongest materials are prone to wear and tear. As cargo shipping containers are used, they bear damage from friction, not to mention collisions from improper handling. There are times when the force of heavy loads adds to the damage as well.

Some of the common damages seen in these units includes twisted frames, pin holes, and cracked welds or seals. Although these can be repaired, it will cost a pretty penny to do so. Additionally, if the damages are not addressed in time, rust may form causing even more problems.

Never forget that these structures have weak areas as well. The thing about steel shipping containers is that they are built to last. Because they are used for imports and exports and are exposed to harsh handling, not to mention weather conditions, and as such they are reinforced on all corners.

But like all structures, these cargo units have their weak spots and one is on the roof. Standard shipping units can only accommodate a limit of about three hundred kilograms at a time. If a homeowner wants a multi-level shipping container home, this imposed but essential limit can easily reduce the potential of converting a space to meet specific living preferences.

Depending on the prospective shipping container homeowner, these cons might be enough to discourage them from making an investment into this housing type, but it is a good thing to know that there are also many benefits to shipping container homes.

Now that all of the potential disadvantages of shipping container homes have been laid out, let us move on to the things that make them beneficial for those who are interested in this type of modern-age residential living.

These days, earning a decent living is hard enough. With plenty of restrictions on income for most people, finding cost-effective alternatives for daily living matters tremendously, and this is one of the main reasons why there are individuals choosing to live in shipping container homes. Compared with other residential options on the market, they offer relatively cheap but desirable accommodations.

Using shipping containers, it is possible to get hundreds of square feet of livable space at a fraction of the price of conventional homes. In the long run, the cost savings exceed rent savings as well. Not bad for owned property. If you are interested in exceptional value for money, this is a home option that you should definitely consider.

Shipping container homes are also some of the most environmentally-friendly buildings available today. From solar panels to energy conserving LED lights, modern times have grown to embrace environmentally friendly products and services.

Shipping container homes are in their own right eco-friendly housing options, as there are thousands of these containers that are recycled into homes. This eliminates the need to manufacture additional building materials to satisfy the residential and commercial development demand. Recycling the steel instead of melting it down or scrapping also reduces the need for energy required for processing.

Building a shipping container home also allows for an efficient construction timetable to be put into play. Because the initial structure already exists, fabricating a residence from shipping containers can be done in a short amount of time as compared with other types of homes.

With an efficient construction timetable means that homeowners get to enjoy their new house faster and have to incur fewer costs to do so. In construction, every day of work translates to significant expenses on labor. It is possible to prepare, build, wire, insulate, and decorate shipping container homes in a few weeks to a couple of months.

Want the structure to be constructed off-site? This is not impossible when it comes to a shipping container home. Shipping container homes can be built on any parcel of land, even an enclosed garage, and can be transported to their final location later on.

This viability for off-site construction is one of the many things that make this residential option extremely appealing. There are instances when certain areas are not conducive for building. This can be because of the limited space, or the unavailability of constant sources of energy making the use of heavy duty power tools hassling.

Access is also relatively easy. When you need a shipping container, it is fairly simple to source one for your build. As countries continue to engage in import and export trading, shipping containers will be readily available. Hundreds of thousands of these containers are used, reused, and repurposed, making the concept of container homes easily justifiable, not to mention highly sustainable.

Because of their primary purpose to transport products across continents, shipping containers have been built to satisfy transportation standards for shipment. Homeowners can easily have these transported via truck, rail, or ship; whichever works best.

You will also benefit from structural durability. Shipping containers are very strong, not to mention durable. Apart from being fabricated from steel, these were designed to stand constant exposure to the elements together with heavy loads and rough handling.

They can stand up to earthquakes and other disasters thanks to their welded modular design. This is why they are excellent materials to use for home construction projects.

Containers easily comply with ISO standards, and have the ability to be stacked in multiple tiers. As they come equipped with built-in interlocking corner supports, fabricating multiple level homes using containers is safe, not to mention easy to do. Those interested in a cost-effective and long-lasting residential solution will find shipping container homes truly beneficial.

Their modular design is another advantage. Shipping containers carry a standard modular design. All containers carry the same width dimensions. In some cases, they differ by height and length, but that is about it.

There are two standard measurements for the latter, so sourcing the right sized containers is still easy. Aside from making residential design planning a breeze, it makes transport as simple as possible too. The modular design can also be attributed to the interlocking quality of these containers.

Their modular design, interlocking components, and built-in support corners reduce the need for additional labor during the home construction process. Homeowners can easily cut costs on steel cutting and welding, to name a few. When it comes to the design process, it only takes simple modifications to make the space adequate for living.

Finally, the limited need for extensive building foundation does not only make builds easy, but fairly cheap as well. There is really no need to spend time on extensive foundational support as basic systems will usually work just fine.

Given these pros and cons of shipping containers, it is up to you to weigh them out and see if a shipping container home is something that will benefit you both in the short and long run.

Chapter 14: FAQs

Still not convinced? Here are some frequently asked questions that may help clarify your other concerns:

1. Aren't shipping containers highly-sensitive to the elements?

Shipping containers, when used to make a home, are insulated just like the walls in any traditional house. This will help with temperature and humidity control.

2. How come shipping containers are hard to buy?

There is a misconception that shipping containers are surplus products. Companies actually reserve them for when they need to have something shipped. Containers that are sold commercially are those which have some age to them. Currently, there is no other way to source these for re-purposing in most places.

3. Can a shipping container be used right away?

Shipping containers sold to the public have often gone through tons of travel and contained various items, some of which may be in liquid form. Potentially a lot of debris has been collected during this time. Pre-treating and thoroughly cleaning these containers, both inside and out, is highly necessary.

4. Are shipping container homes rust-proof?

These containers are made from durable Corten steel which is coated with ceramic paint. This makes them resilient against rust and corrosion.

5. Why should I live in a home that looks like it came from the shipping yard?

Just like other building materials, the container will serve as the foundation for your home. You can then decorate it anyway you like both internally and externally. Depending on your preference, you can choose to cover it in other materials like wood or stucco that will make it unrecognizable as a shipping container.

6. Do all neighborhoods allow these types of homes?

There are building codes and zoning regulations that different communities must follow. Be sure to check with local authorities on whether or not this type of home is permitted in your area.

Conclusion

Thanks again for taking the time to read this book!

You should now have a good understanding of shipping container homes, and be ready to start working on designing and building your very own!

If you enjoyed this book, please take the time to leave me a review on Amazon. I appreciate your honest feedback, and it really helps me to continue producing high quality books.

www.ingramcontent.com/pod-product-compliance
Lightning Source LLC
Chambersburg PA
CBHW061058050726
47592CB00004B/1729